# Stabilizing the Mind

A Meditational Technique to
Develop Spaciousness in the Mind

## JETSUNMA AHKÖN NORBU LHAMO

wild dakini
PUBLISHING

Wild Dakini LLC
P.O. Box 304
Poolesville, Maryland 20837 USA
www.wilddakini.com

Copyright © Jetsunma Ahkön Norbu Lhamo 2019

All rights reserved. No part of this book may be reproduced in any form electronic or otherwise, without written permission from Jetsunma Ahkön Norbu Lhamo.

Second edition
Printed in USA

ISBN 978-09855245-0-0
Ebook ISBN 978-0-9855245-7-9
1. Meditation 2. Buddhism

Library of Congress Control Number: 2019931569

Stabilizing the Mind
by Jetsunma Ahkön Norbu Lhamo

Cover photo by Sonja Peter depicts rock formations in Central Australia

Cover and book design by Jane Perini Middleton

*It is within the nature to reveal to yourself
the place that is beyond conceptualization...
underneath conceptualization...
like the crystal under the dust.*

*This book is dedicated to the
long life of Jetsunma Ahkön Norbu Lhamo
and the long lives of His Holiness Karma Kuchen
Rinpoche and all masters of the Palyul Lineage.*

We acknowledge with gratitude Jane Perini Middleton for her contributions of design and editing to the production of this book on meditation. Also, thanks to Sonja Peter from the Australian sangha who photographed the image for the cover that so perfectly shows both stability and spaciousness; and Ani Dianne Cadwallader for her support in bringing this publication to fruition. Our thanks to Michael Brunk and Kristin Laing for their attention to detail in the final edits. While there are a few changes in this edition, the teaching remains as it was first printed, a perfect guide from beginning meditation to experiencing the natural state.

We take full responsibility for any errors or mistakes that were made in the course of preparing this book.

May this book be of benefit.

Ani Rinchen Khandro and Ani Tenzin Wangmo
Wild Dakini Publication Coordinators

# CONTENTS

FOREWORD | 7

INTRODUCTION | 9
How I Began to Practice

CHAPTER 1 | 13
Why It's Hard to Stabilize the Mind

CHAPTER 2 | 19
Two Practical Approaches for Developing Spaciousness

CHAPTER 3 | 25
Stepping Back from Reaction

CHAPTER 4 | 31
How to Get Ready to Meditate

CHAPTER 5 | 35
How to Watch Your Breath

CHAPTER 6 | 39
How to Disengage from Distracting Thoughts

CHAPTER 7 | 47
Ask Yourself "Who is Meditating?"

CHAPTER 8 | 51
Developing the Habit of Going to an Abstract Place

CHAPTER 9 | 55
When Does the "I" Begin and When Does It End?

CHAPTER 10 | 61
Emptiness is Not Cold, Dark and Empty

CHAPTER 11 | 67
The Steps Build on Each Other

CHAPTER 12 | 71
Learning to Reside in a State of Innate Wakefulness

AFTERWORD | 77
Becoming Firm in Your Practice

MY WISH FOR YOU | 81

DEDICATION | 83

GLOSSARY | 84

ABOUT JETSUNMA AHKÖN NORBU LHAMO | 86

# FOREWORD

Her Eminence Jetsunma Ahkön Lhamo Rinpoche is one of the great living masters of the Palyul lineage on this planet who has been teaching Buddhadharma for several decades. She is none other than the reincarnation of the great yogini Mandarava, who was the consort of Guru Padmasambhava. She is an authentic Bodhisattva, born in the West, who has boundless love and compassion toward all sentient beings.

In the 21st century, we are all very busy and focused on the eight worldly concerns, such as name and fame and so on. We don't have much time for in-depth study and practice. From her vast compassion and wisdom, Her Eminence Jetsunma Akhön Lhamo Rinpoche has presented traditional Buddhist teachings in a way that will help us immensely with practice and contemplation.

I am very grateful to be part of this amazing book called *Stabilizing the Mind*. I wish and pray that this book will bring great benefit to all the Western people. May it benefit whoever reads it, contemplates it, and meditates on it. May all sentient beings be free from the ocean of suffering. May all sentient beings attain complete enlightenment in this very life.

Khenpo Pem Tsheri Sherpa
Namdröling Monastery

INTRODUCTION

# How I Began to Practice

*There are certain tried-and-true methods in the Buddhist tradition that are extremely useful, but I would like to tell you about my own early experience.*

How do we stabilize the mind? There are certain tried-and-true methods in the Buddhist tradition that are extremely useful, but I would like to tell you about my own early experience.

When I started to meditate as a teenager, I didn't know there were books about meditation, because there weren't metaphysical bookstores where I was, and I didn't know of anybody who was practicing meditation.

I started meditating all by myself. I always knew that I would do something spiritual with my life, and I was always waiting for the signal that would tell me the time had come. I knew that there would be a time when there would be a signal. I got the first signal when I was nineteen. Three times within a couple of weeks I had a dream of a scene in front of the house on the farm where I was living. In the dream, the sky was very, very black, incredibly black, like no other thunderstorm I had ever seen. And there was a white truck in front of the house and two other little cars and some odd things. And it seemed that I was standing on the porch. Each time I had the dream, I heard a voice say to me, "When you see this, then things are changed, and you should begin." It still gives me chills to talk about it.

The day after I had that particular dream for the third time, we had some company. They came in cars and one came in a white truck, but I just did not connect the vehicles to the dream. After I had finished cooking and putting things away, and everybody was relaxing, I thought I would go out on the porch for a breath of fresh air. I looked up and noticed that a tremendous storm was coming in. The sky was incredibly black, and the clouds were moving in. I thought, "Oh, yes." Suddenly I looked forward, and there was that scene from my dream. And I remembered the voice saying to me, "When you see this, then things are changed, and you should begin." The scene was so grabbing. There were different things lying on the lawn—toys and different strange things that did not belong to us. It was too unusual, too precisely like that dream, to miss it. So I thought, "Okay. Well, here we go. Things are changed now. I wonder what that means." So I went inside and I told everyone I was going to take a nap. I just laid down and tried to comprehend what was happening.

I knew that I would get help, so I just asked, "What do I do first? How does one meditate?" At each point, I got very excellent instruction. Very precise. Just the right thing. And it wasn't just a sit-down-and-calm-your-mind meditation. It wasn't like that at all. It was almost scientific. It was very exacting, very much like the Buddhist teaching that details specific things that you must do—how you should sit, how you should breathe, how you should visualize, how you should dissolve into emptiness.

The reason why I'm telling you my story is so that you don't think I'm making a claim that I am teaching you something out of a Buddhist text. I am not. I am teaching you something that came from my own mind and that I found very helpful and that I felt was very successful. Since I've had Buddhist teachings, I know the technique is based on the same principles that the Buddha taught. So you can label it any way you wish.

CHAPTER 1

# Why It's Hard to Stabilize the Mind

*We have a habit of
not being able to break away
from the entrancement of our lives.*

Even though many of us practice the Dharma and consider ourselves to be Buddhist practitioners, it is obvious that many of us do very little to try to stabilize our minds. Although we practice sincerely, somehow something falls through the cracks; we don't see that we're not doing the best we can to stabilize our minds.

I've really studied this situation and examined all of the phenomena that make this happen. I think, first of all, that it is very painful to look at ourselves. It's like being hooked into TV. We can't take our eyes away from the action; we can't stop watching. We remain fixated on the TV. Even if someone talks to us, we say, "Huh? Yeah, yeah…," and keep watching.

Well, we are like that about the continuum in our lives. You may have noticed that life takes on a cyclic appearance. There tend to be periods of activity and periods of introspection—periods when we tend to be more aware. Everyone notices this differently. Some people may notice that their lives are very active some of the time and then more introspective. Some people may notice that they are more aggressive at certain times and more passive at other times. Some people may notice that they are more objective some times and more subjective at other times. How we think of ourselves depends on our particular vocabulary and how we relate to the activity in our life.

When we are in an active phase, or an aggressive phase, or an objective phase, a phase in which there is a great deal of visible movement—not internal movement necessarily, but visible movement—we do not stop. We have a habit of not being able to break away from the entrancement of our lives. We can't stop in the middle of it. It is during that active phase that we usually make our worst mistakes, when we get the most unstable. During that active phase, we let ourselves roll with whatever comes along.

When that cycle is over—and it is very individual whether that cycle lasts ten minutes, an hour, a day or longer—we may wake up and wonder, "Where have I been for the last while? I have been in Gaga-Land somewhere. But I've been very busy." That is when we come home, like a pigeon, in our own particular way. At that time, there is a period of inactivity, an inward feeling. At that time, it is relatively easy to stop and look at how we have been thinking, what we did that was wrong, what we did that was right, and how it all relates to practice.

The difficult habit to break, then, is to be able to pull ourselves away from the TV, to use that process of introspection in the middle of an active or aggressive phase. That skill is hard to master because, in order to have that skill, one needs a little space in the mind. There must be some mental spaciousness.

Both the cause and the effect, or the phenomenon that results from the cause, takes place within our mind. When there is spaciousness, there is a moment's pause between them, so that we can connect the fact that effect is the result of cause.

Now most human beings, during the more passive, introspective times can look and see cause and effect in their lives. Animals cannot do this. Their learned behavior is different from ours. They do not understand cause and effect. But like Pavlov's dog, they can learn to react to certain stimuli, but there is no space in their minds. They are floating on a sea of sensuality, on sensory input. They have no awareness that these events occur within their minds or that they have causes. The fact that we know cause and effect shows that we have some spaciousness within our minds. It does not necessarily mean, however, that those who are most logical and most reasonable have the most space in their minds.

CHAPTER 2

# Two Practical Approaches for Developing Spaciousness

*We have to develop the habit of
putting some spaciousness into our mind
in order to accomplish spaciousness
at the time of our death.*

The trick, then, is to try and break the entrancement, or the habit in the middle of an active phase, so that we can really have space at all times—not just in the introspective points—in our lives. Why is this so important? Well, for instance, let's get practical and look at the moment of death. The moment of death could come at any time. At any moment, a truck could come barreling down the driveway, go right through this room, and knock all of us out. We all could be goners. Is it possible? Sure, it's possible. Such things can happen, and when they happen, it may not necessarily be at a time when we are in a spacious place, at a time when we can recollect or look. The moment of death could come at a time when we are profoundly entranced.

If we had time to plan for our death—for instance, if we were told, "You're having a heart attack, and you're probably going to die within an hour"—we would have a better shot at being shocked into an introspective place, where we could have some space in our mind. But it isn't necessarily so. There's no telling how we will react to the awareness that we are dying. Most people actually die without being aware that they are dying. They might die in their sleep and not register what is happening to their body at the time, or they might have an accident that results in instantaneous death.

Because they may not have an opportunity to do any of the things that one is supposed to do at the moment of death, there's no spaciousness there. You have to develop the habit of putting some spaciousness into your mind in order to accomplish spaciousness at the time of your death. That is one practical application.

Another reason for developing this kind of spaciousness is that we need to begin to disengage some of the habitual tendencies that are associated with samsara, or cyclic existence. We may already know this, and many of us are planning to do this someday in our practice. We are planning to rid our minds of hatred, greed, and ignorance sometime. We may think that we are working toward it now, but we have really decided that we won't practice seriously until sometime later. And so, basically, we are content to live with hatred, greed, and ignorance. In other words, we let ourselves get away with murder. We let ourselves get away with temper tantrums, pride, and arrogance.

And so what happens, then, is that although we are practicing Dharma—and we're continually practicing—at the same time we are incurring more and more negative karma. In effect, we're working against ourselves, spinning our wheels in the middle of nowhere. It's not useless, but it's not productive either. It's a very difficult situation.

So, another practical reason why we need space in our minds is to aid our practice, so that the practice into which we are putting a lot of time can be productive and useful, and so that we can get the most out of it. The goal of practice is to rid the mind of desire. So ask yourself: is it logical to exist comfortably with our desire, our pride, our hatred, our greed, and our ignorance without trying to do something about it now?

No one can get rid of desire, get rid of pride, or get rid of anger if there is not enough stability and spaciousness to look at what is in one's mind, to see how we are acting and to see what it is going to bring about. There must be a little space to be able to do that. Otherwise, we will be one of those people who says, "But I can't help it. I always get arrogant... I always get mad. I'm compulsive." By saying, "I always do that," and "I can't help it," that is saying that you are comfortable with your behavior and you are willing to live that way.

That attitude does not accomplish anything a practitioner wants to do. Once we have adopted the goals of Buddhism and are working on the path to enlightenment, it does not make any sense to coexist with these faults comfortably and to let them be. And so, we have to do something about ourselves.

CHAPTER 3

# Stepping Back from Reaction

*We need to begin to stabilize the mind by sensing the difference between our nature and our conceptualizations—the wonderful, artful designs that we surround ourselves with...*

In order to develop spaciousness in the mind, in order to develop some kind of stability, we have to find a way to step back from reaction. Some people seem to react instantaneously. Other people appear to react after they've chewed on something and discovered something distasteful. Whichever type we are, the reaction actually always comes automatically and instantaneously, even for those people who tend to ruminate on things and take a while to show their reaction. For those who get hot quickly, they simply see it right away and feel it right away because there is less of a time lapse. With the other kind of person, the same process happens, but it takes more time for the reaction to surface—even though the actual reaction begins immediately.

Somehow, we have to be able to step back from our own minds long enough to be able to watch these reactions, to be able to see where they come from. If we can't watch ourself do it, if we cannot take a step back from it, we will never have any success mastering our moods. We have to be able to master our emotions to progress toward enlightenment.

How do we step back from our own minds? The reason why we think it's so tricky, and the reason why we think it can't be done, is because we think we are our brain. We think that's all we are, and we don't even know that we think that. Sentient beings just assume that what they perceive is correct, and determine who they are by their reactions toward what they perceive. Whatever we are feeling—attraction or repulsion— that is the thing by which we measure ourselves. Basically, we think that these perceptions that we have, these reactions that we have, these things that we gather around ourselves, are us. And, of course, that is the fundamental problem of beings caught in samsara.

We often ask ourselves again and again: "Why do I do this to myself?" "Why do I make myself suffer?" "Why do I go through what I go through?" "Why can't I be happy when I really want to be happy?" And the answer is that we don't know our own nature. What we think we are is not what we are at all. Unless we have practiced deeply, we have never tasted our nature, not even for an instant, and that is the problem. Some people may have had experiences of one kind or another that point the way, that show there is something in store at some point, but that is not the same as having an experience of one's nature.

So, we need to begin to stabilize the mind by putting space in the mind, by sensing the difference between our nature and our conceptualizations—the wonderful, artful designs that we surround ourselves with, the perceptions that we have and the reactions that we have. We have to somehow have enough space to be able to tell that the things we surround ourselves with are not necessarily our own nature.

So how can we begin to do that? Before we talk about how we can begin to do that, I want to apologize if it seems like I am belaboring a point or trying to sell you on why we need space in our minds. I can almost hear some of you saying, "But I already know that I need space in my mind. Just give me the technique."

In fact, there is one person who always says, "Just tell me how to do it." I listen to that and I think that, without question, in almost every case, the very person who says, "Just tell me how to do it," or, "Just give me the technique," is the very one who does not understand why it is important to have space in the mind.

I am not convinced that any of us are really sold on how important it is to stabilize the mind. You can see the evidence by just watching people in their lives. It is incredible to me to see how much we let ourselves get away with. It's unbelievable to me how much pride we still have, how much we are willing to live with that pride, and when we're reproached, how easily we bounce back with excuses as to why we should have that pride. It is amazing to me how we are willing to allow ourselves to be hateful, to be angry, to be moody, to be all of these things and not question ourselves or not make any kind of on-the-spot effort to rectify the situation. Most amazing of all is how often we sell out, how many compromises we make.

The sellout factor is incredible in sentient beings. We are willing to think that it is okay to hate, because we have a reason. We're willing to think it is okay to be angry, because we have an enemy. We're willing to think that it is okay to give this much and not too much more, because we have other things to do. We think it is okay to act inappropriately, to speak inappropriately, or disrespectfully, to not deal correctly with our practice. We just make up all these different reasons why it's okay; we defend ourselves in that way. So if I belabor the point, it's because it is important to realize it is within everyone's power to overcome pride and to overcome the negligence with which we deal with our spiritual practice, with our life.

CHAPTER 4

# How to Get Ready to Meditate

*Be patient with yourself.*

In order to stabilize the mind, you must sit very still. You cannot do this technique lying down. You should find a position in which you can sit comfortably for a long period of time without being distracted by bodily aches and pains. If you can, sit in a cross-legged position, because there are some benefits to sitting in this way, such as leaving open certain energy passageways and helping to keep the spine fairly straight. But there is no real reason why you can't do the same procedure sitting in a chair.

Sit with the spine as straight as possible. Look at your posture. If you are bow-backed, you still have to find a way to sit so that the spine is straight, even if it means you have to sit against something that is straight. If you are sway-backed, as I am, you may have to position a pillow under your bottom in such a way that your chassis is balanced, so that the spine doesn't bow in one direction or another.

Make sure you are not constricted in any way. If your clothing is tight, you may want to loosen it. I found that to be very useful. You should also sit with your hands in your lap, just gently relaxed.

Once you are in position, allow yourself to relax completely and breathe normally. At first, when you tell yourself to breathe normally, you are going to breathe abnormally because you're going to be convinced that you are suffocating, that you're not getting enough air. And you'll start breathing like a horse, like you've been running a mile. So you have to get past that. You have to learn to be relaxed, to breathe normally and to put your attention on your breath. When you are breathing normally, it is common to breathe in through your nose and out through your mouth. It may take you a few sessions just to breathe naturally and deeply, without tension. Be patient with yourself.

CHAPTER 5

# How to Watch Your Breath

*The point is to breathe naturally and to put only the gentlest, gossamer-thin attention on your breath.*

The first step is to learn to breathe naturally and to watch the breath at the same time. Now to watch your breath, put a very light attention on your breathing. Get away from the tendency to control your breathing; just breathe naturally in whatever way you are used to breathing. The point is not to have a health experience. The point is to breathe naturally and to put only the gentlest, gossamer-thin attention on your breath. It is like taking your pulse; you don't press down hard. You watch it just barely. The attention is not overbearing or overpowering; it's almost like you're riding on the surface of your breath with your consciousness. You barely observe it, and you observe it very passively without making any judgments. After you concentrate gently on your breath for a few sessions, you can learn to become almost feathery in that concentration on your breath.

It is good to spend a few weeks, or at least a few days, just watching the breath. In the beginning, as you practice this technique, you must give yourself some time to learn how to watch the breath without struggling, and with attention that is like a feather, like a butterfly wing. As long as you are working toward mental stability—and watching the breath provides mental stability—there is no real hurry. In one way, all sentient beings have hopes of us achieving realization so that their suffering will be ended, but on the other hand, why rush? It's like burning the candle at both ends.

The big skill at first is learning not to fall asleep. If you have difficulty staying awake, do not make excuses. Do not say, "I don't have a lot of energy, so when I sit still I always fall asleep," or "I'm not well," or "I'm an active person and I'm not used to sitting still." If you find yourself getting sleepy, re-establish your mindfulness of compassion, remembering that you are meditating in order to attain realization to be of benefit to sentient beings. It is not so that you can be bored. We are supposed to be accomplishing a goal. We allow that strong concern for others to be enough of a fire in our hearts that this becomes the most important thing for us.

We stay awake when we are brushing our teeth; I have never met anybody who fell asleep brushing his teeth. We stay awake when we are washing our cars. We stay awake when we are vacuuming. We care about our teeth; we care about our cars; we care about our floors. We have to learn to care that much and more about sentient beings. So much more that, for their sake, we will practice. And that really is what keeps us awake after a while. So long as we remain really fixated on ourselves and absorbed in ourselves, all we will notice is that we are sitting still and that it is a good time for a nap. But when we are truly concerned for the well-being of sentient beings, we will practice for their sake.

CHAPTER 6

# How to Disengage from Distracting Thoughts

*You will hear that chatterbox going all the time, and the knack is to realize it has always been there and there is no need to follow it down the road.*

Your mind is used to being active, and your mind is going to throw thoughts at you while you're watching your breath. It does not want you to meditate. The trick here, the thing that is difficult, is not to follow your inner voice, the noisemaker in your head, down the road. The chatterer is going to try to distract you, and you are going to be distracted. And when you are distracted, you should handle it by simply disengaging.

Here is what is going to happen when you are distracted: Your brain will throw a thought at you, and you will concentrate on that thought, and you'll notice that this thought goes somewhere. It develops itself in a linear progression, and you follow it. What happens when you are following the voice down the road is a lot of conceptualization, a lot of contrived view, belief and opinion—all kinds of attraction and repulsion, action and reaction.

Once you become skilled at putting your attention on your breath, you will hear that chatterbox going all the time, and the knack is to realize it has always been there and there is no need to follow it down the road. The voice will keep talking as it always does, and you'll get caught on little phrases that you hear in your head, but your meditation is lost, not by hearing it, but by following it down the road.

Do not try to suppress the voice in your head. You should not argue with it at all. In fact, simply let it be. You should not make any judgments about what the voice is saying, especially if the thought is about how good you are. You should not agree with it or disagree with it. You should not notice when it is there and when it is not there. You may be aware of it, but you simply do not engage. But don't think, "I'm not going to think now." Don't think, "Calm your mind." And, for goodness sake, do not use positive thoughts. I can't believe that people still do that, but they do. Do not say, "I'm going to be empty now," "I'm going to be blissful." Please don't do that. Thoughts will still come.

In fact, once the little guy realizes that you are not paying any attention to him, he is going to get louder. And he is going to try little tricks, like screaming "The pot is boiling!" or "You left the iron on!" or "The house is blowing up!" or "You're having a heart attack!" The little guy is just going to try to drive you out of your mind. Well, that is exactly what you shouldn't let him do. What you want to do is to remain passive and learn how not to follow the chatter, learn how to simply have a gossamer-thin attention on the breath. Each one of you will develop your own skill at doing this.

One way is to sensitize yourself to knowing when you have followed the chatter down the road. There is some point at which you know you must have followed the chatter because you are not simply watching the breath; you are down the road somewhere. When you're down the road, don't say, "Oh nuts, I'm down the road again." When you're down the road, don't say, "Well, I just can't meditate." When you're down the road, don't say, "You got me again." Simply disengage.

Disengaging is a good skill that we all need to learn. Try

visualizing tongs or spaghetti holders picking up the thought and then dropping it. Really, you may have to get graphic at first to disengage. The point is to drop the thought, to let it go wherever it's going to go. Even drop the judgment of whether it's a good thought or a bad thought. Drop it and come back to the focus of gently watching the breath. Every time you get off the mark just the least little bit, disengage.

Now, you may say, "Gee, I don't want to spend all my time doing that." But watching the breath is the beginning of stabilizing the mind. You are doing something useful; you are learning to break that cycle of activity. You are learning to put some spaciousness in your mind. Even if you can only disengage at the moment of death, your practice will have been successful.

Little by little, and it takes time, you will find that the distance that you run down the road with the chatter will become shorter and shorter. And the way to do that, again, is to disengage the moment you realize you are down the road and not centered on the attention on your breath. Do not even look at the thought you are dropping. Simply drop it. I am emphasizing this point so much because it is the hardest thing to do. It really is tough to learn to just drop it, because we believe we have to examine our garbage before we dump it.

Now when those thoughts start developing in a linear progression, when they go down the road, they are going to be trance-like, like a TV set from which it is hard to break away. The tendency will be to say, "Let's see what's happening here." Forget "Let's see what's happening here," because that is going to take you further down the road. Just let go. That moment of letting go is a skill that is a tremendous help in your meditation.

So you will be practicing to disengage faster and faster, until at some point, almost like a sphincter, you can feel yourself tightening around a thought that comes up, disengaging from it almost immediately, so you are not following it at all. That is really important. Eventually you will be able to do that, but it may take some time. Give yourself the time you need to do this.

Do not judge how you are doing. Don't think, "Well, gee, I'm worse today than I was yesterday." Or, "I'm worse this week than I was last week." There are so many different factors in making the mind active or clingy or whatever it is doing. There are so many different variables. There are so many different ways in which we respond to our lives.

Even once one becomes a very good meditator, at some point there will be times when you simply cannot let it go; you simply cannot meditate very effectively that day. Then there is a point, of course, when you can always meditate; but at that point, so many things have changed already. Our response to phenomena has changed. We have had some perception of the natural state, the mind is relaxed, the medicine is doing its job.

Even if you have begun to practice this technique for only a week, the medicine is already beginning to work. It doesn't matter if it seems like we're worse the next week. Our job is to do this thing passively, to do it without making a lot of judgments about ourselves. And that's the hardest thing to do. It is really hard not to make judgments about ourselves and our progress.

At some point, the impulse to follow the voice down the road will actually go away. The voice will become so minimal as to be essentially nonexistent. Eventually, as one gets closer and closer to realization, what makes up the voice begins to change, and the whole scenario changes.

The most important thing is to not get impatient with yourself, to learn to watch the breath in a gossamer-thin way, to do it in such a relaxed state that when the chatterer wants to take you down the road, you can let go without any entrapment. You can simply let go. That's the big skill. That is very important. Once you find that you can remain in meditation and not follow the voice down the road, you will find that the mind is in a very relaxed state and there is a lot of what we call spaciousness in the mind.

When thoughts come up, learn to let them go almost like bubbles popping on the surface of a pond. Just let the thoughts pop. Do not follow them. Do not even look to see what they are. The thoughts will still come up, but you can get to the point where your attention on them is so short-lived that you almost don't look to see what they are. All the time you are developing better and better your ability to just have a very gentle awareness of your breath.

CHAPTER 7

# Ask Yourself "Who Is Meditating?"

*Do not think you are going to learn how
you feel about yourself at this time,
because that is not the point.*

Now, once you get to that point of stability and the thoughts are going away quickly, you have learned to disengage. You have not learned to stop thinking—you don't have a stable mind yet—but you have learned to disengage. At that point, introduce the next step.

After doing the breathing meditation for some period of time—maybe a half-hour or an hour—ask yourself, "*Who* is meditating?" or "*Who* is watching the breath?" You are not going to be so out of it that you can't ask yourself a question. I know that some of you think, "Oh no, I'll be in bliss, I won't be able to disengage." Trust me. You'll manage.

So allow yourself to look at who is watching the breath. Now what is going to arise in the mind is a set of circumstances, pictures, those things that make up the conceptual understanding associated with "I." These things will come up; try to view them gently, as gently as you watch your breath—without any judgment, without any persistence. Gentleness is important here. It doesn't matter if the concepts that come up when you ask the question, "Who is watching the breath?" are crystal clear, because the first thing you are going to say is, "I am." There is a concept that makes up "I." "I" is not just a little letter drawn with one line; "I" is a concept. That is really how it works in our minds. And when

"I" comes up, a lot of stuff is going to come up with it. Do not get psychological. Do not think you are going to learn how you feel about yourself at this time, because that is not the point. Do not try to figure out how you feel about yourself. If "I" comes up and "I" feels like a terrible disgusting person, do not analyze it. If "I" comes up and "I" feels like the Second Coming, do not analyze it. No matter how "I" comes up, do not analyze it. Just view it as concepts surrounding "I." One by one, begin to let the concepts drop away.

For some of you, those concepts will be crystal clear, because that is the kind of person you are: I am old, I am young, I am big, I am little, I am fat, I am thin, I am smart, I am not smart. Whatever your concepts may be, dissolve them. Do not try to make them vague or big or weird or anything; dissolve them one by one.

For some of you the concepts will not be crystal clear. They will be very vague. If they are vague, do not try to crystallize them. Do not try to make them succinct. Do not try to make them anything. Just let them fall away. Don't think that you have to know what is falling away. You don't. And don't isolate the concept; that is making it stronger. You want to dissolve it.

So one by one, allow your concepts of "I" to dissolve. The concepts will keep coming up one after another, and you will find that there is concept after concept, after concept, after concept. Go all the way in.

After doing this for some time, little by little, you will go more and more in, in, in. It will feel like "in" to most people. It is uncharted ground here; there is no book written on this. You will feel like you are going in—or something like that—but it will become more and more essential, more and more abstract.

CHAPTER 8

# Developing the Habit of Going to an Abstract Place

*...like the crystal under the dust.*

Soon, you will begin to develop the habit of being able to go into a very abstract place. There is a point at which you will experience a feeling of just "suchness" without any definition. Even when you experience that, as long as you can say, "I'm feeling suchness now," go in more. Even when you go in more and you say, "I'm a little beyond suchness now," go in more. Even when you have gone all the way in and you say, "Well there's certainly nothing here now," go in more. So long as there is anything left of your brain to make waves, you keep going in. It is not really in your body, you understand? It is within the nature to reveal to ourselves the place that is beyond conceptualization, underneath conceptualization, like the crystal under the dust. After a while, you will develop more and more of the skill of getting to that place that is free of, or underneath, conceptualization.

This, then, is one way to stabilize your mind. You should get so strong in this meditation that you can do it at any time. You can do it in the middle of the worst pain, even in child-birth. You should practice doing it at the drop of a hat, instantly. You can even make a game of it: Instantly, whoosh! Kind of like that.

Practice disengaging at a moment's notice. Practice doing it midstream, even if you are in the middle of a compulsion. And if you are a person who never finishes anything, do it after you finish. Stop all the time and practice in that way.

Then, after you get really good at this practice, and you feel that you are having some success in disengaging your mind, you can go into a place that seems to be pre-conceptualization, or under conceptualization.

CHAPTER 9

# When Does the "I" Begin and When Does It End?

*The thing that makes you "you"
is something that is very transient.*

The next thing you want to do is to remember that there were concepts or ideas that came up when you asked yourself, "Who is watching the breath?" Now you are going to recall that you had those conceptualizations, and you are going to think to yourself that there was a time when the "I" that you thought of, and have been aware of most of your life, began, and there will be a time when it ends.

You should think to yourself, "What is the time that I begins and what is the time that I ends?" When do you begin? You begin at your birth. Right? I mean, you might have been something else before that, but you begin at your birth. You could have been protoplasm, you could have been an amoeba, you could have been a frog. But at your birth you became you.

Then, while you have a light attention on your breath, you allow the thought to permeate into your awareness that the "I" you are talking about is merely a circumstance. Remember you're in control here; you're not running away with thoughts! You already have the sense of "suchness." You already have the sense of "beyond conceptualization."

Now you must also have the sense that this nature that you are beginning to sense is not the same as the thing that began at birth. Look at the time of your birth and the circumstances surrounding it. What seems to make you you, is the time of birth, the idea that you began at that time. You are going to explore the ideas that surround the self. But you are going to do it as though you're on top of a building and you're watching people meet on street corners beneath you. You are way up there observing.

Now you are not thinking about your moment of birth, but about this person whom you have discovered, have taken all of the proliferations away from, have swept clean and discovered suchness underneath. What started all of that?

You are going to discover concepts such as, "'I' started at the time of my birth and 'I' will end at the time of my death." The thing that makes you "you" is something that is very transient. What is it? Look at what it is. You are going to discover that it is concepts. It is ideas. It has to do with time and space.

From the point of view of suchness, or natural awareness, look at those circumstances that determine your ego, that determine your birth and your death, that determine all the things that you know about yourself, that determine your fate. See that they are merely concepts; they are ideas and they are not the same as that suchness. And yet, they are not separate from that suchness. You really have to play with that. When did it start? When will it end?

After you discover that concepts determine the "I-ness" that you thought you had—and again you are looking at this from a distance and from a state of relaxation, light attention and awareness of a pure nature—you are going to have a very different perception of "you". It is very hard for me to tell you what you are going to see, but it is going to seem very different.

The last part of this contemplation for right now is to have a sense of before the time of birth, before that "you" continuum began, to see if you can sense if there was any awareness before the time of birth.  At the time of birth, as you came in through the "I-ness" that you think you are, you began to gather impressions, concepts around yourself—and all of the many different things that you saw come up at first: I'm short, I'm tall, I'm fat, I'm skinny, I'm old, I'm young, I'm this, I'm that." What came before?

The danger here is fabrication. That is why this step should be the last step, after you have developed some skill. All of us can have a fabricated experience that precedes our birth; but it's not a true experience. What you are trying to do is to experience that there was something, some awareness before the persona "you"— whoever you are—continuum began to develop, to evolve in its linear fashion. Please do not make any determination such as, "I was a little ball of light," or "I was in darkness. They called me out." Please, don't do any of that funny stuff. Just get a sense that there is something that precedes these conceptualizations.

You should have that sense long enough to realize this: that the nature that you are, that you have discovered, that you have uncovered after you have swept away all the conceptualizations, is empty of self-nature. You are somewhere underneath all the things that define self, free of conceptualization, empty of self-nature. By so doing, you will realize that the nature of emptiness and the nature of all phenomena in your mind are the same, and you will begin to feel a sense of control.

CHAPTER 10

# Emptiness Is Not Dark, Cold and Empty

*Your job is to discover that emptiness is not empty at all.*

When we say that all things are essentially empty, what we mean is that all things are empty of self-nature. All things are empty of conceptualization. Conceptualization is just junk that happens; it is the stuff with which we surround ourselves. It is empty of self-nature, but it is not dark and cold and empty. Fullness and emptiness without conceptualization are exactly the same. The nature and the phenomena that we produce are exactly the same when you take the concept out of them. It is only concept of this and that—concept of self-nature and concept of "other"—that makes them appear separate. But this and that, full and empty, light and dark are the same taste. Our job, then, is to discover that emptiness is not empty at all, and yet it is "no thing." Not nothing.

If these practices are done faithfully, a little space begins to develop in the mind, a little freedom, a little working room and some stability. Once this meditation technique is mastered, even if one masters just point one and point two—one can begin to fight one's moods, one's anger, hostility and pride. The tendency to have an ego as big as a barn can be overcome. We will find that we can fight the tendency to do all of the things that we do so well that are so much against the Buddha's teachings. We can fight our tendency to go through something and then be ashamed of ourselves later. We can fight the tendency we have to simply react and to live in a world of reaction. We can put a little space between our minds and the knee-jerk reactions that occur with conceptualization. Things *seem* to happen automatically because our minds are tight, like rubber bands. We pull them back and they snap.

We do have the power and the space and the tools to make ourselves what we want to be. And as practitioners, hopefully what we all want to be is a person with a stable enough mind so that we can surely reach enlightenment in order to benefit beings. That is the name of the game. That is why we want to practice in this way. We are not meditating to be pacifists; we are meditating to be in control, to have stable minds. In this practice, when we get to the place of pure awareness, we will already have a clue that it is not cold and dark emptiness, because even at that place, there is tremendous joy. It is not a joyful *thing*, because it is not a "something." We cannot say, " 'I' feel joy in this place." But once the walls are gone, there is the natural expanse of pure luminosity, and it is not unhappy. It doesn't have the constriction of unhappiness. It is not shut in. It's like having shoes on that were too tight, and you just took them off, and your feet are stretching out. Your toes are wiggling and you are getting some air on your feet. It's like an "Oooooooh! Yeah!"

Depending on our metabolisms, we are going to feel it differently, in our own way. But we will have a sense that it is not dark and cold and empty. When we are stuck in the belief, the religion of ego, we think that we are all of these constraints that we have put on ourselves. Really, in that state we think we are our shoes! And that is a really sad place to be. All the proliferations with which we surround ourselves are not what we are. Once we realize this, there is a tremendous sense of freedom.

The game is to get control, to get stability, to get freedom, and to get close to doing what we came here to do—not wait until the last moment when we are 50-odd years old. Start practicing now. Begin to gain some control now.

CHAPTER 11

# The Steps Build on Each Other

*You have to be truthful with yourself. Please do not think you are ahead of where you are.*

The steps in this meditation technique all build upon each other. To do the second step you have to do the first step. To do the third step you have to do steps one and two. Do not try to do all three at the beginning. You will be tempted to think that you can. Trust me. You can't. You have to develop the first step in a very stable way. The first step is hard to develop. Even disengaging, even watching the breath without panicking, all of these things take time.

We may think that we can disengage, but we can't because we are still down the road. We have to be truthful with ourselves. Please allow yourself enough time. Please do not think you are ahead of where you are. One of the biggest faults I see in some of the people that need this practice the most is that they think that they are so much further ahead of where they really are. That worries me a little bit. So, please, give yourself time. I did step one for a few months before I was given the directive to go on. Maybe you can gauge by that how long you should do the first part. I don't know. But after I did the first part for a few months, I practiced the first and second parts as my sole practice for a long time, and then went on to the third part.

After I practiced step three for a few months, I began to have spontaneous awareness or realization of my own nature as I was walking around. It was very often and very spontaneous, and I would almost feel a sense of disorientation. This may not happen to you; it could be just something peculiar to me.

For example, on the farm there was a beautiful bubbling stream. I remember listening to the water and becoming absorbed in the water because it was really gurgling. There was ice forming on the sides. Suddenly I had an awareness of that state that is free of conceptualization, of that suchness, of that natural awareness; and as that natural awareness, I suddenly realized that I could have been and was the water. So I found myself looking at the world from the water.

For those of us who think we have had that experience, we must realize that there is a difference between that kind of experience and the mind playing tricks, or our pretending that we are somewhere else—a kind of mental projection that is nowhere near the same kind of experience. One must have a stable mind and one has to be able to disengage in order to have a sense of that suchness. But that is the kind of experience each of us can have, with practice.

CHAPTER 12

# Learning to Reside in a State of Innate Wakefulness

*...simply let it go, realizing
all things are an emanation of mind,
realizing all things are constructed.*

There is another technique that we can use after we learn to breathe naturally and follow our breath at the same time. Because I used this technique before I ever heard of Buddhist practice, I am going to give it in the way that it came to me.

First, I would concentrate on my breath and have light attention on the breath, and I would stabilize my mind through that means. After I had developed the skill of letting thoughts go without following them down the road, I would watch my breath, allowing myself to rest in that awareness. Then I would put my attention just lightly on the perception of the world—all the phenomena around me. And I would dissolve that phenomena. Just dissolve it. Again not forcefully—not: "You go away!"—but very gently. The feeling I had was of simply allowing it not to be, of letting it go, as though I recognized it was my own construction in the first place.

There seemed to be some intermediate energy between me and phenomena. I could sense energy surrounding me, almost as though I were experiencing the energy of my own mind or something like that. You may not experience that. In that case, this part is optional. But I did experience it, and I am trying to tell you exactly how I practiced. I would also dissolve that intermediate energy. I would simply let it go, realizing that all things are an emanation of mind, realizing that all things are constructed. Then I would perceive my own body in the way that I perceive it, and again, I would allow the body to dissolve.

I would perceive my own mind full of the perceptions, the qualities and the different events that occur within the mind, and I would dissolve that also. I would continue to dissolve until there was a state that was naturally awake. This state was not dead and cold. It had the quality of innate wakefulness, but it was not "something" or "anything." I would dissolve all of the constructions that I made; I would dissolve and simply rest in that innate wakefulness. When that happens, thoughts will bubble up, almost like bubbles and ripples coming to the surface of a pond. The moment that they come up, let them dissolve without letting them take you down the road. Keep developing that skill until you are doing it automatically and consistently, and you learn how to reside in that state that is uncontrived, that is pure of conceptualizations and pure of construction of any kind. Develop a sense of experiencing a natural or an awakened state.

There is a danger here. We cannot let ourselves get carried away with the joy. If we do, the little chatterer is going to take us down the road again. So we have to learn to reside peacefully in this state. And we have to develop the skill of allowing the joy or the happiness that arises not to be about a perception such as "I'm happy I did this," or "I'm happy I'm feeling this way," or "This must be close to what Buddha taught,"— none of those things. We simply have to learn to reside with gossamer attention on that happiness so that it is very peaceful. That takes skill.

I always found that when I arrived at that state—I am not saying that I did it on a regular basis—and having allowed myself to experience that, there were moments of tremendous joy, almost bliss. It was like experiencing nature without a girdle on, without the things that we put the wisdom nature in, without the contrivances. It seemed like suddenly I could breathe. There was almost a sense of flight.

AFTERWORD

# Becoming Firm in Your Practice

*Looking at your mind in some stable way so that you can understand that the mind just floats helplessly, constantly, on its own concepts and that these concepts are the cause for suffering, and that there is no lasting happiness in them, gives you a firm foundation.*

When we come to understand what the Buddha and all the great lamas have taught, we will come to understand that it basically boils down to the fact that all sentient beings are suffering, that desire is the cause of suffering, that there is an end to suffering, and that end is enlightenment.

There are different ways that we can attain enlightenment, but they all have to do with ending attachment and desire in the mindstream. They have to do with realizing that our nature is not the same as the conceptual proliferations that we live with, or the desire that we live with, or the egos that we perceive as ourselves.

Once we understand enough so that we can look at our lives—with all of the emotional highs and lows—we realize that everything is impermanent, and that we are just riding on our own concepts. We become aware that by doing so, we can't make our minds stable enough to break free of the compulsion to revolve in cyclic existence for aeons and aeons, that awareness becomes the taskmaster. That realization becomes the teacher.

If we do not realize that circumstances are impermanent, if we are practicing because we have some crazy idea that we're going to be "great beings" some day, or that we are going to triumph in the end and that it is all about self and self-cherishing, if we have some romantic notion about ordination or about practicing at all, we will never be stable in our practice.

Understanding the teachings about impermanence is the stabilizer, the real teacher. Understanding from the depth of our hearts that desire really is the cause of suffering, is the taskmaster. Looking at our minds in some stable way so that we can understand that the mind just floats helplessly, constantly, on its own concepts (whichever way the concepts go, up or down) and that these concepts are the cause for suffering, and that there is no lasting happiness in them, gives you a firm foundation. It is then that we understand why we practice, and although the circumstances of our life may change, at that point, we will never turn away from practice. We may go to work or we may stay home, we may have children or we may not, we may take robes or we may not—whatever the circumstances are of our lives—as long as we know these things, we will remain firm.

Being infatuated with the culture, with the music, with the color, and with the ritual of Tibetan Buddhism will never be enough. We must understand the heart of the Buddha's teaching and the value of compassion. We each have to understand how important it is to end suffering and what the means are to end suffering in order to stay with the Dharma, in order to be stable and safe in the Dharma.

# My Wish for You

It is my sincere hope that this little book will provide a measure of comfort and perhaps some clarity on the path. The teachings collected here are given in such a way that they relate to our lives, our experience. I like to teach this way, so that the instructions are not externalized—or thought of as something that does not touch us, affect us.

It's easy to hear Dharma, if we have the merit. It's easy to keep a record of how many teachers in whose presence we have sat. It is much harder to change, to remain where we are and to deepen. It is harder still to rely on the advice of our Spiritual Master rather than on our own prideful, rigid, ordinary ideas.

The path of Dharma must renew for us a profound, living presence in our lives. It should never become stale or stiff, nor should we allow our minds to become hard, rigid or prideful. We should hold our hearts and minds in a confident posture of trembling, joyful expectancy. Then the path becomes our treasure, our food, our refuge. Then, gradually, we transform into that most precious jewel, the aspirant who actually gives rise to the Bodhicitta, who makes love and compassion a living presence in the world. This is the answer to all our longing.

May the power and potency of Dharma fill our lives. May virtue prevail. May compassion be born in our hearts and devotion nourish our minds, pouring forth to all sentient beings who remain in samsara. May they be liberated from the very causes of suffering.

And may it be soon; may it be today. May samsara be emptied. Lord Guru, of the suffering of sentient beings, there has been enough. I dedicate all virtue I have accomplished, in this and every other lifetime, past, present and future, to this end.

– Jetsunma Ahkön Norbu Lhamo

# DEDICATION

*By this effort
may all sentient beings
be free of suffering.
May their minds be filled
with the nectar of virtue.
In this way may all causes
resulting in suffering be extinguished,
And only the light of compassion
shine throughout all realms.*

Jetsunma Ahkön Norbu Lhamo

# GLOSSARY

**Bodhicitta:** The mind of enlightenment that encompasses wisdom and compassion.

**Buddha:** The historical founder of Buddhism, Shakyamuni. Also, one who is completely awake to his or her true nature and the true nature of all reality.

**Conceptualization:** Perception, thoughts and reason are all concepts in our mind to identify objects perceived physically or mentally as separate from oneself. (See also 'Self-nature' in this Glossary.)

**Dharma:** The pure path taught by the Buddha that leads one out of suffering into the awakened state of enlightenment. Dharma is the underlying meaning of the Buddha's teachings; the truth upon which all Buddhist practices, scriptures and philosophy are based.

**Emptiness:** The complete absence of true existence in all phenomena.

**Enlightenment:** The cessation of suffering reached when the qualities of compassion and wisdom are perfected and all non-virtue has been extinguished from one's mind.

**Ignorance:** One of the main causes of suffering along with hatred and greed; a lack of awareness of cause and effect relationships.

**Karma:** Universal law of cause and effect governing the activity of unenlightened beings, whereby all experience is the result or fruit of some previous action or cause. Through the force of intention we perform actions with our body, speech, and mind, and all of these actions produce effects. The effect of virtuous actions is happiness and the effect of negative actions is suffering.

**Meditation:** Encompasses various forms of mind practice to increase spiritual awareness. There are two principal forms of meditation practice: the development of concentration and the development of insight.

**Samsara:** The endless round of death and rebirth, characterized by impermanence, cause and effect, suffering, and ignorance of true reality.

**Self-nature:** Ego structure.

**Suchness:** The fundamental, natural state.

# About Jetsunma Ahkön Norbu Lhamo

From an early age, Jetsunma Ahkön Norbu Lhamo has devoted herself to meditation and the alleviation of suffering in the world. With confirmation from two highly revered Tibetan Buddhist masters, His Holiness Dilgo Khyentse Rinpoche and Dzongnang Rinpoche, His Holiness Penor Rinpoche, 11th throneholder of the Palyul Lineage in the Nyingma tradition, recognized Jetsunma as a reincarnation of the 17th century yogini Genyenma Ahkön Lhamo. The first Ahkön Lhamo was the sister of Rigdzin Kunzang Sherab, the founder and first Throneholder of Palyul.

Subsequently, His Holiness Kusum Lingpa recognized Jetsunma as an emanation of Princess Lhacham Mandarava, the Indian consort of Padmasambhava (also known as Guru Rinpoche, or Precious Teacher), the Indian scholar who stabilized Buddhism in Tibet. Jetsunma is the first Western woman to have been officially recognized and enthroned as a Tulku, an enlightened being who reincarnates in whatever form necessary to benefit sentient beings.

With innate compassion and wisdom, and drawing on her

experiences as a Western woman, Jetsunma makes even the most profound Buddhist teachings accessible. Her teachings, often infused with humor, reach a broad audience, including long-time Buddhist practitioners as well as people simply wanting to live with kindness and generosity. Jetsunma encourages each of us to create a world of compassion, by contemplating the suffering of others, and taking action to bring about change.

In *Stabilizing the Mind*, Jetsunma Akhön Norbu Lhamo takes a practical approach to meditation borne of her awareness that people's minds are in a constant state of distraction. In the first chapters of the book Jetsunma describes techniques that prepare and calm the mind. This provides a foundation for the more advanced meditation practices introduced in the later chapters of the book.

# *Other books and music by Jetsunma!*

## BOOKS

Viewing the Guru Through the Lens of the Seven Limb Puja

Vow of Love

Boundless Treasury of Blessings:
A Collection of Prayers, Teachings and Poems

## MUSIC

### Revolution of Compassion
*A unique brand of smooth socially conscious electronica, infused with traditional Tibetan mantra and chants. Genre: Electronic: Illbient*

### Delog
*A smooth, down tempo mix of urban trip hop infused with ancient Tibetan mantra and chants, this eclectic CD brings an edge to enlightenment. Genre: Electronic: Trip Hop*

### Ellinwood Ranch Blues
*Jetsunma's vocals, one part earthy and emotional, two parts smoky and sultry, combine with her powerful lyrics and trademark universal messages as she explores new musical territory with the blues. Genre: Blues: Blues Vocals*

### Trilogy
*A spiritual center of funk, blues, R&B, new age alternating with sounds of jazz. Genre: World: World Beat*

### Remixes
*Lyrics that call for change are woven with Buddhist mantra and set to electronia and dance beats. Genre: Electronic: Dance*

---

Books available through major retailers and music on all music platforms. For more information: *https://www.tibetanbuddhistaltar.org/books-and-music/*

www.ingramcontent.com/pod-product-compliance
Lightning Source LLC
Chambersburg PA
CBHW040209020526
44112CB00039B/2848